feeling
ill?

Allergies

By Jillian Powell

Contents

WHAT'S WRONG?

Allergies can cause skin rashes, sneezing, wheezing and sickness. An allergy is when your body reacts badly to something. You can be allergic to different things, like some foods or medicines. They are called **allergens**.

Dear Doc

My Mum gets hay fever. Does it mean I will get it too?

Some allergies run in families. You may have a skin-prick test *to see if you have an allergy.*

If you have an allergy, your body treats the allergen like a germ. It makes **antibodies** to fight it. As they fight, they make **histamines**. These cause allergy symptoms.

FOOD ALLERGIES

Some people have a food allergy. You can be allergic to any kind of food. Cow's milk, eggs, nuts, soya beans and **shellfish** are all common allergens.

Food allergies can cause a rash, itchy eyes, wheezing and upset stomach. In a bad allergic reaction, the tongue and mouth can swell up and make it hard to breathe.

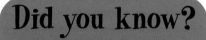

Did you know?

Food additives can cause allergies. You can check labels to see which additives foods contain.

I have a nut allergy. Mum checks all the labels when we go shopping. Lots of foods have tiny bits of nuts in them. They could make me ill.

HAY FEVER

Hay fever is an allergy to plant pollen. You may sneeze, have a blocked or runny nose, itchy eyes and sometimes headaches. Some people are allergic only to grass or tree pollens.

Dear Doc

I get bad hay fever at exam time. What can I do?

Avoid going outdoors, especially if anyone is mowing the grass.
Try hay fever tablets but make sure they are the non-drowsy type!

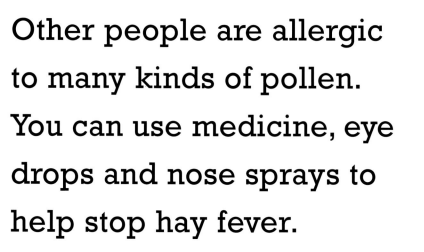

Other people are allergic to many kinds of pollen. You can use medicine, eye drops and nose sprays to help stop hay fever.

Did you know?
You can check the pollen forecast on tv or radio to find out how high the *pollen count* is each day.

11

HOUSE DUST MITES

Some people have an allergy to **house dust mites**. They are tiny mites that live in our homes. They leave droppings that can get into the air. If you breathe them in, they can cause a runny nose, sneezing and sometimes allergic **eczema** or **asthma**.

Dear Doc

I am allergic to house dust mites and I often wake with a blocked nose. What can I do?

Use special covers to keep dust out of your duvet and pillows. Wash them on a hot wash and vacuum the bed when you change it.

Keeping the home clean and dust-free helps. Wooden floors or tiles are better than carpets.

PET ALLERGIES

Some people have allergies to pets. Mostly, they are allergic to animals with fur or feathers.

Leo's story

My Nan has a cat called Mittens. When I went to stay with her, I was always coughing. I found out I was allergic to cats. Now, Nan makes sure Mittens is out when I go to visit!

14

These pets leave **dander** in the air, which can make it hard to breathe.

Anti-histamine medicines can help if you have an allergic reaction to pets.

15

INSECT ALLERGIES

Some people are allergic to insect bites and stings, which make their skin swell up and get red and itchy. If they have a bad allergic reaction, their tongue can swell up and it may be hard to breathe. They need medicine to make them better. This is sometimes injected with a special pen.

Dear Doc

I have to carry adrenalin *injections* with me in the summer because I am allergic to bee stings.

How do I use it?

You inject it into your thigh so the medicine goes into a muscle.

A wasp stung me when we were having a picnic. It got inside my drink! My mouth swelled up. I had to have an injection to make it better.

SKIN ALLERGIES

Some people have a skin allergy. They can get a rash from plants, washing powders or some jewellery. Pollen, dust and some foods can also cause skin allergies.

Eczema is a red, itchy or sore rash. You can use creams to help make it better.

Dear Doc

I can't stop scratching my eczema. It's so itchy. What can I do?

Eczema creams can help. Try not to scratch as eczema can get infected. Then you may need antibiotics *to clear it up.*

I kept getting an itchy rash. The doctor told mum to try changing her washing powder and I stopped getting the rash.

STAYING HEALTHY

If you have an allergy, you should try to avoid the allergen as much as possible. Clean, fresh air is good for people with allergies that affect breathing. They should avoid smoke and pollution.

I wear this Medic-Alert bracelet because I am allergic to the drug **penicillin**. If I get ill, it warns the doctor not to give me any.

You should wear a **Medic-Alert** to warn people that you have an allergy to a food or medicine.

Did you know?

Pollution may be causing more people to get allergies.

Glossary

Allergens	substances that can cause allergies
Allergies	when the body reacts badly to something
Antibiotics	drugs that kill germs
Antibodies	substances that the body makes to fight germs or allergens
Asthma	breathing problems like wheezing and coughing, sometimes brought on by allergies
Dander	tiny bits of skin and hair from animals
Eczema	an itchy, red rash on the skin
Food additives	colours, flavours and other substances added to packaged foods
Histamines	chemicals that the body releases when it is fighting an allergen
House dust mites	tiny mites that live in soft furnishings
Injection	using a needle or special pen to put medicine into the body
Labradoodles	a breed of dog that is a mix between a poodle and a labrador
Medic-Alert	a medical warning usually worn on jewellery
Muscle	a type of tissue in the body that we need for making movements
Non-drowsy	describes a medicine that does not make you sleepy
Penicillin	an antibiotic drug
Pollen count	the amount of pollen in the air, usually higher in warm dry weather
Pollution	dirt in the air or ground caused by cars and factories
Shellfish	seafoods with shells, such as prawns and mussels
Skin prick test	a test used to find out if someone is allergic to something